Words of Hope

Words of Hope

CONNIE HARRISON

ELEMENT

Shaftesbury, Dorset • Rockport, Massachusetts

Published in Great Britain in 1991 by
Element Books Limited
Longmead, Shaftesbury, Dorset

Published in the USA in 1991 by
Element, Inc
42 Broadway, Rockport, MA 01966

Cover illustration 'Sunrise' by Max Hermann Pechstein 1881–1955
Courtesy of the Saarland Museum,
Saarbruken/Bridgeman Art Library
Cover design by Max Fairbrother
Calligraphy by Connie Harrison
Printed and bound in Great Britain by
Billings Ltd, Hylton Road, Worcester

British Library CIP data available
Library of Congress data available

ISBN 1–85230–238–0

In Memory of Paul.
May Love like Sunlight
surround you.

INTRODUCTION

This book was written
and is sent to you with love.
It seems we need
to experience pain before
we can truly understand
ourselves and the suffering
of others.
Our thanks must go out
for the words of wisdom
and truth given by seers
and poets of all races
and religions, which give
comfort and support
in the midst
of life's traumas.

It is my hope
they will bring
comfort, and help you
to understand more fully
any painful situation
through which you may be
passing.

ACKNOWLEDGEMENTS

The compiler acknowledges with gratitude the courtesy of the following individuals and companies in permitting the use of copyright material. For Bible version, see under the general heading 'Bible'.

Anon, (Go to a Tree), reproduced by kind permission of Men of the Trees (a registered charity), Sandy Lane, Crawley Down, West Sussex RH10 4HS.

Marcus Aurelius, *Meditations*, transl. Maxwell Staniforth (Penguin Classics, 1964, pp. 108, 178), © Maxwell Staniforth, 1964, reproduced by permission of Penguin Books.

Richard Bach, *Illusions: The Adventures of a Reluctant Messiah*, Pan Books Ltd, 1978, by permission of Macmillan, London and Basingstoke.

Extracts from the Authorised Version of the Bible (the King James Bible), the rights in which are vested in the Crown, are reproduced by permission of the Crown's patentee, Cambridge University Press.

Bible: New English Bible (2nd edn). © 1970 by permission of Oxford and Cambridge University Presses.

Scripture quotations from the Revised Standard Version Bible, © 1946, 1952, 1971, by the Division of Christian Education of the National Council of the Churches in Christ in the USA and used by permission.

Caddy, Eileen, *The Living Word*, 1977 reprinted by permission of the Findhorn Press.

Feild, Reshad, *A Travelling People's Feild Guide*, 1986, reprinted by permission of Element Books.

Grenfell, Joyce, *Joyce: by Herself and Her Friends*, 1980, reprinted by permission of Macmillan, London and Basingstoke.

Gyatso, Geshe Kelsang, *Joyful Path of Good Fortune*, Tharpa Publications, London, 1990. By permission of Geshe Kelsang Gyatso.

Haich, Elisabeth, *The Day with Yoga*. © 1983, Aurora Press, Santa Fe.

Julian of Norwich, *Revelations of Divine Love*, ed., Betty Radice, transl.

My first thanks go to my
husband Paul, for the strength
he gave me in life
and whose death
brought this little book
into being.
Grateful thanks to
my teachers,
past and present.
Loving thanks to my daughter
Carol for her support
in many ways.

Thank you also to Shirley
and Edward Clunies-Ross,
Evie Spenn, Joyce Winstanley,
Margaret Hampton, Inge
and Timmy Crump, Molly
Hanford and many friends
who have suggested,
supported, helped
and comforted.

What the caterpillar
calls the end of the world
the master calls a butterfly.

RICHARD BACH

Take therefore no thought
for the morrow:
for the morrow
shall take thought
for the things of itself.
Sufficient unto the day--

AUTHORISED VERSION BIBLE
Matthew 6.34

What did Enlightenment
bring you?

Joy
And what is Joy?
The realization
that when everything is lost
you have only lost a toy.

ANTHONY DE MELLO

Every human being
is a spark that wants
to burst into flame.

RESHAD FEILD

Ask, and it will be given you;
seek, and you will find;
knock, and it will be opened
to you.

REVISED STANDARD VERSION BIBLE
Matthew 7.7

How great a being,
Lord, is Thine,
Which doth all beings keep!
Thy knowledge
is the only line
To sound so vast a deep.
Thou art a sea
without a shore,
A sun without a sphere;
Thy time is now
and evermore,
Thy place is everywhere.

JOHN MASON

After a while you learn
the subtle difference
between holding a hand
and chaining a soul.
And you learn that love
doesn't mean leaning
and company
doesn't mean security.
And you begin to learn
that kisses aren't contracts
and presents aren't promises.
And you begin to accept
your defeats with your head up
and your eyes open
and with the grace of an adult,
not the grief of a child.

And you learn to build
all your roads on today
because tomorrow's ground
is too uncertain for your plans.

After a while you learn
that even sunshine burns
if you get too much.
So plant your own garden
and decorate your own soul
instead of waiting
for someone to bring you flowers
`` And you will learn
that you really can endure –
that you really are strong.
And you really do
have worth. ''

ANONYMOUS

Consider the lilies
of the field,
how they grow;
they toil not,
neither do they spin:

AUTHORISED VERSION BIBLE
Matthew 6.28

Except a corn of wheat
fall into the ground and die,
it abideth alone;
but if it die,
it bringeth forth much fruit.

AUTHORISED VERSION BIBLE
John 12.24

Caring is the greatest thing,
caring matters most.

FREIDERICH VON HUGEL

But every morning
the day is reborn
among the
newly-blossomed flowers
with the same message retold
and the same assurance
renewed that death eternally
dies, that the waves
of turmoil are on the surface,
and that the sea of tranquillity
is fathomless.
The curtain of night is drawn
aside and truth emerges
without a speck of dust
on its garment,
without a furrow of age
on its lineaments.

RABINDRANATH TAGORE

And this our life,
exempt from public haunt,
finds tongues in trees,
books in running brooks,
sermons in stones
and good in everything.

WILLIAM SHAKESPEARE

Music to the Deaf.

I used to be stone deaf.
I would see people stand up
and go through
all kinds
of gyrations.

They called it dancing.
It looked absurd to me
—until one day
—I heard the music!

ANTHONY DE MELLO

You are already what
you are searching for,
since
what you are
looking for
is what is
looking.

RESHAD FEILD

Earth's crammed
with heaven
And every common bush
afire with God,

But only he who sees
takes off his shoes.

ELIZABETH BARRETT BROWNING

Set the bird's wings with gold
and it will never again
soar in the sky.

RABINDRANATH TAGORE

"How shall I help the world?"

By understanding it
said the Master.

"And how shall I
understand it?"

By turning away from it.

"How then shall I
serve humanity?"

By understanding yourself."

ANTHONY DE MELLO

To all life Thou givest,
to both great and small;
In all life Thou livest,
the true life of all;
We blossom and flourish
as leaves on the tree,
And wither and perish—
but nought changeth Thee.

WALTER CHALMERS SMITH

Sometimes
there would be a rush
of noisy visitors
and the silence
of the monastery
would be shattered.
This would upset the disciples;
not the Master
who seemed just as content
with noise
as with the silence.
To his protesting disciples
he said one day,
"Silence is not
the absence of sound,
but the absence of self."

ANTHONY DE MELLO

Every person,
all the events of your life
are there
because you have
drawn them there.
What you choose
to do with them
is up to you.

RICHARD BACH

The Disabled Fox.—A fable
of the Arab mystic Sa'di:

A man
walking through the forest
saw a fox
that had lost its legs
and wondered how it lived.
Then he saw a tiger
come in
with game in its mouth.
The tiger had its fill
and left the rest of the meat
for the fox.
The next day God fed the fox
by means of the same tiger.

The man began to wonder
at God's greatness
and said to himself,
"I too shall just rest
in a corner with full trust
in the Lord
and he will provide me
with all
I need."
He did this for many days
but nothing happened,
and he was almost
at death's door
when he heard a voice say,
"O you who are in the path
of error,
open your eyes to the truth!

Follow the example
of the tiger
and stop imitating
the disabled fox."

ANTHONY DE MELLO

The butterfly has leisure
to love the lotus,
not the bee
busily storing honey.

RABINDRANATH TAGORE

O master poet,
I have sat down at thy feet.
Only let me make my life
simple and straight,
like a flute of reed
for thee to fill with music.

RABINDRANATH TAGORE

The stag in the fable
admired his horns
and blamed his feet;
but when the hunter came,
his feet saved him,
and afterwards,
caught in the thicket,
his horns destroyed him.
Every man in his lifetime
needs to thank his faults.

RALPH WALDO EMERSON

Do not linger
to gather flowers
to keep them, but walk on,
for flowers
will keep themselves blooming
all your way.

RABINDRANATH TAGORE

Life is full when
you are empty.

RESHAD FEILD

They that love
beyond the world
cannot be separated by it.
Death cannot kill
what never dies.

WILLIAM PENN

Love is a mind
that wishes all other beings
to be perfectly happy.

GESHE KELSANG GYATSO

Love is patient; love is kind
and envies no one.
Love is never boastful,
nor conceited, nor rude;
never selfish,
not quick to take offence.
Love keeps no score of wrongs;
does not gloat
over other men's sins,
but delights in the truth.
There is nothing
love cannot face;
there is no limit to its faith,
its hope, and its endurance.
Love will never come to an end.

NEW ENGLISH BIBLE
1 Corinthians 13.4-8

Fearlessness

"What is love?"
"The total absence of fear,"
said the Master.
"What is it we fear?"
"Love,"
said the Master.

ANTHONY DE MELLO

Shall I compare thee
to a summer's day?
Thou art more lovely
and more temperate;
Rough winds do shake
the darling buds of May,
And summer's lease
hath all too short a date:
Sometime too hot
the eye of heaven shines,
And often is his
gold complexion dimmed:
And every fair from fair
sometime declines,
By chance,
or nature's changing course,
untrimmed:

But thy eternal summer
shall not fade
Nor lose possession
of that fair thou owest;
Nor shall Death brag
thou wanderest in his shade
When in eternal lines
to time thou growest.
So long as men can breathe,
or eyes can see
So long lives this,
and this gives life to thee.

WILLIAM SHAKESPEARE

'Love seeketh
not itself to please,
Nor for itself hath any care,
But for another gives its ease,
And builds a Heaven
in Hell's despair.'

WILLIAM BLAKE

Were the whole realm
of nature mine,
That were an offering
far too small;
Love so amazing,
so divine,
Demands my soul,
my life, my all.

ISAAC WATTS

Accept with love
the flaws of your friends
and enemies,
and you may learn
to love and accept yourself.

RESHAD FEILD

There is nothing wrong
with loving ourselves.

RESHAD FEILD

I came to offer thee a flower,
but thou must have
all my garden
It is thine.

RABINDRANATH TAGORE

Immortal Love,
for ever full,
for ever flowing free,
for ever shared,
for ever whole,
A never-ebbing sea.

JOHN GREENLEAF WHITTIER

Let my love,
like sunlight,
surround you
and yet give you
illumined freedom.

RABINDRANATH TAGORE

Green grape, ripe cluster,
raisin; every step a change,
not into what is not,
but what is yet to be.

EPICTETUS

'Be ye transformed
by the renewing
of your minds.'

A snake cannot grow
Without shedding
its old skin
A baby chick cannot emerge
from its shell
Without cracking it open
A baby cannot be born
Without emerging
from its mother's womb.

EILEEN CADDY

To every thing
there is a season,
and a time to every purpose
under the heaven:
A time to be born,
and a time to die;
a time to plant,
and a time to pluck up
that which is planted;
A time to weep,
and a time to laugh;
a time to mourn,
and a time to dance.

AUTHORISED VERSION BIBLE
Ecclesiastes 3.1, 2, 4

Even in the center
of the very greatest cyclone
there is absolute stillness.

ELISABETH HAICH

Humankind learns much
faster through adversity.
If everything is easy and
no obstacle is in our way
we never learn anything.

ELISABETH KÜBLER-ROSS

And when the earth
shall claim your limbs,
then shall you truly dance.

KAHLIL GIBRAN

You get what you need,
you always get
what you need
you don't always get
what you want.

ELISABETH KÜBLER-ROSS

We shrink from change;
yet is there anything
that can come into being
without it?
What does Nature hold dearer,
or more proper to herself?
Could you have a hot bath
unless the firewood
underwent some change?
Could you be nourished
if the food suffered
no change?
Is it possible
for any useful thing
to be achieved
without change?
Do you not see, then,

that change in yourself
is of the same order,
and is no less necessary
to Nature?

MARCUS AURELIUS

God promises
a safe landing
but not
a calm passage.

BULGARIAN PROVERB

"Calamities can bring growth
and enlightenment,"
said the Master.
And he explained it thus:

Each day
a bird would shelter
in the withered branches
of a tree
that stood in the middle
of a vast deserted plain.
One day a whirlwind
uprooted the tree
forcing the poor bird
to fly a hundred miles
in search of shelter—

till it finally came
to a forest
of fruit-laden trees.

And he concluded:
"If the withered tree
had survived,
nothing would have induced
the bird to give up its security
and fly."

ANTHONY DE MELLO

The wounded oyster
mends its shell
with pearl.

EMERSON

There is no such thing
as a problem
without a gift for you
in its hands.

You seek problems
because you need
their gifts.

RICHARD BACH

For, lo, the winter is past,
the rain is over and gone;
The flowers appear
on the earth;
the time of the singing of birds
is come—

AUTHORISED VERSION BIBLE
The Song of Solomon 2.11-12

All things
are subject to change
and are no lasting refuge.
Fundamentally
they are but illusions
with no permanent substance.
By recognising this truth
we can stop clinging
to this world
and so set ourselves free
to act in accordance
with our true nature
which is limitless compassion
love and wisdom.

REV DAISHIN MORGAN

The flower sheds all its petals
and finds the fruit.

RABINDRANATH TAGORE

One may not reach the dawn
save by the path of the night.

KAHLIL GIBRAN

All the trials of life
are meaningless
unless
you learn from them.

Man was made
for joy and woe;
And when this
we rightly know,
Thro' the world we safely go.
Joy and woe are woven fine,
A clothing for the soul divine;
Under every grief and pine
Runs a joy
with silken twine.

WILLIAM BLAKE

The source of suffering
is our sense of self,
which is out of harmony
with the universe,
which is selfless.

AJAHN TIRADHAMMO

Much of your pain
is self-chosen.
It is the bitter potion
by which the physician
within you heals your sick self.
Therefore trust the physician,
and drink his remedy
in silence
and tranquillity:
For his hand,
though heavy and hard,
is guided by the tender hand
of the Unseen,
And the cup he brings,
though it burn your lips
has been fashioned
of the clay

which the Potter
has moistened
with His own sacred tears.

KAHLIL GIBRAN

The young deer,
wandering among
The Summer green
and pleasant ways,
Remembering his mother
caught And killed
in a trap,
can yet enjoy
The freedom
of the empty valley
And find relief
and rest of mind.

CHÖGYAM TRUNGPA

When you are in pain,
it's hard to remember
that everything that happens
is to teach you something
and be grateful for it.

RESHAD FEILD

I have a pearl
to give to you who weep
whose beauty's born
from simple life
and fashioned out of pain
it fills a mandala
with space to breathe
and gently gathers light
it is not struck from rock
or circled like a diamond noose
to bind you by
but free and perfect
grew unknown
where nature turns
invading pain
to beauty and delight
So hold it fast

and catch the spread of sunrise
in the single point of light.

MARGARET TORRIE

God is our refuge and strength,
a very present help in trouble.
Therefore will not we fear—

AUTHORISED VERSION BIBLE
Psalm 46.1, 2

My clouds,
sorrowing in the dark,
forget that they themselves
have hidden the sun.

RABINDRANATH TAGORE

Love is not changed
by Death,
And nothing is lost
and all in the end
is harvest.

EDITH SITWELL

Death is not the
extinguishing of
the light, but the
putting out of the
lamps because the
dawn has come.

RABINDRANATH TAGORE

And if tonight my soul
may find her peace in sleep,
and sink in good oblivion,
and in the morning wake
like a new-opened flower
then I have been
dipped again in God,
and new-created.

D.H. LAWRENCE

If I should go
before the rest of you,
Break not a flower
nor inscribe a stone.
Nor when I'm gone
speak in a Sunday voice,
But be the usual selves
that I have known.
Weep if you must,
Parting is hell,
But life goes on,
So sing as well.

JOYCE GRENFELL

For what is it to die
but to stand naked
in the wind
and to melt
into the sun?
And what is it to cease breathing
but to free the breath
from its restless tides,
that it may rise
and expand
and seek God
unencumbered?

KAHLIL GIBRAN

The Salt Doll

A salt doll journeyed
for thousands of miles
over land,
until it finally came to the sea.

It was fascinated
by this strange moving mass,
quite unlike anything
it had ever seen before.

"Who are you?"
said the salt doll
to the sea.

The sea smilingly replied,
"Come in and see."

So the doll waded in.
The farther it walked
into the sea
the more it dissolved,
until there was only very little
of it left.
Before that last bit dissolved,
the doll exclaimed in wonder,

"Now I know what I am!"

ANTHONY DE MELLO

"DEATH is nothing at all.
I have only slipped away
into the next room.
I am I, and you are you.
Whatever we were
to each other,
that we still are.
Call me by my old
familiar name,
speak to me in the easy way
which you always used.
Put no difference in your tone,
wear no forced air
of solemnity or sorrow.
Laugh as we always laughed
at the little jokes
we enjoyed together.

Pray, smile,
think of me, pray for me.
Let my name
be ever the household word
that it always was,
let it be spoken
without effect,
without the trace
of a shadow on it.
Life means all that it
ever meant.
It is the same as it ever was;
there is unbroken continuity.
Why should I be out of mind
because I am out of sight?
I am waiting for you,
for an interval,

somewhere very near,
just round the corner.
All is well."

CANON HENRY SCOTT HOLLAND

Faith is the bird
that feels the light
and sings when the dawn
is still dark

RABINDRANATH TAGORE

I have seen thee.
In the face of a child,
In the blossoms
on bare branches,
In the moonlight
and the sunset.
I have seen thee.

I have heard thee.
In the song of a bird
In the laughter
of children at play
In the wind
and the rain.
I have heard thee.

I have felt thee.
In the touch of a friend
In the warmth of the sun
upon my face.
In the waters
and the gentle breeze.
I have felt thee.

I have been with thee.
In joy and sadness
In the long and sleepless night
I have felt thy love
and know that all is well
I have been with thee.

ANONYMOUS

Go to a Tree

When you grow weary
of the boasts of men,
Go to a tree my friend—
one that has stood
Long patient years
within a silent wood.
Beneath its branches
you will find again
A thing long lost,
trees are content to be
As God created them.
No bough that turns
its golden thoughts
to autumn ever yearns
Beyond a hillside's
immortality.

Go to a tree in silence,
you will find
In the soft eloquence
of bud and leaf
Serenity beyond the voice
of grief
And faith beyond the reach
of humankind.
Man spends his noisy days
in search of gain
While trees find God
in sunlight,
soil and rain.

AUTHOR UNKNOWN

Lo, I am with you alway,
even unto the end
of the world.

AUTHORISED VERSION BIBLE
Matthew 28.20

Nevermore thou needest
seek Me;
I am with thee everywhere;
Raise the stone,
and thou shalt find Me;
cleave the wood
and I am there.

HENRY VAN DYKE

I have seen death too often
to believe in death.
It is not an ending
but a withdrawal.
As one who finishes
a long journey,

Stills the motor,
Turns off the lights,
Steps from his car,
And walks up the path
To the home that awaits him.

DON BLANDING

The Lord is my shepherd;
I shall not want.
He maketh me to lie down
in green pastures:
he leadeth me
beside the still waters.
He restoreth my soul:
he leadeth me
in the paths of righteousness
for his name's sake.
Yea, though I walk
through the valley
of the shadow of death,
I will fear no evil:
for thou art with me;
thy rod and thy staff
they comfort me.

Thou preparest a table before me
in the presence of mine enemies:
thou anointest my head
with oil;
my cup runneth over.
Surely goodness and mercy
shall follow me
all the days of my life:
and I will dwell
in the house of the Lord for ever.

AUTHORISED VERSION BIBLE
Psalm 23

Faith is an oasis
in the heart
which will never
be reached
by the caravan
of thinking.

KAHLIL GIBRAN

I saw Eternity the other night
Like a great Ring
of pure and endless light,
All calm,
as it was bright...

HENRY VAUGHAN

The eternal God
is thy refuge,
and underneath
are the
everlasting arms.

AUTHORISED VERSION BIBLE
Deuteronomy 33.27

Abide in me, and I in you.
As the branch
cannot bear fruit
of itself,
except it abide in
the vine;
no more can ye,
except ye abide in me.

AUTHORISED VERSION BIBLE
John 15.4

The year's at the Spring,
And day's at the morn;
Morning's at seven;
The hill-side's dew-pearled;
The lark's on the wing;
The snail's on the thorn:
God's in his heaven—
All's right with the world!

ROBERT BROWNING

Drop Thy still dews
of quietness,
Till all our striving cease;
Take from our souls
the strain and stress,
And let our ordered lives
confess
The beauty of Thy peace.

JOHN GREENLEAF WHITTIER

He makes
the wounded spirit
whole,
And calms
the troubled breast.

JOHN NEWTON

Glory be to God
for dappled things—
For skies of couple-colour
as a brinded cow;
For rose-moles
all in stipple
upon trout that swim;
Fresh-firecoal chestnut-falls;
finches' wings;

GERARD MANLEY HOPKINS

The Japanese warrior
was captured by his enemies
and thrown into prison.
At night he could not sleep
for he was convinced
that he would be tortured
the next morning.
Then the words
of his master
came to his mind.
"Tomorrow is not real.
The only reality is now."
So he came to the present —
and fell asleep.

The person over whom
the future has lost its grip.
How like the birds of the air
and the lilies of the field.
No anxieties for tomorrow.
Total presence in the now.
Holiness!

ANTHONY DE MELLO

Thou wilt keep him
in perfect peace,
whose mind
is stayed on thee:
because he trusteth in thee.

AUTHORISED VERSION BIBLE
Isaiah 26.3

All
shall be well,
and all shall be well,
and all manner of thing
shall be well.

JULIAN OF NORWICH

Peace I leave with you,
my peace I give unto you:
not as the world giveth,
give I unto you.
Let not your heart be troubled,
neither let it be afraid.

AUTHORISED VERSION BIBLE
John 14.27

Still, still with Thee,
when purple morning breaketh,
When the bird waketh,
and the shadows flee;
Fairer than morning,
lovelier than the daylight,
Dawns the sweet consciousness,
I am with Thee.

HARRIET BEECHER STOWE

We come from Thee and to Thee we return.

there is continuity---

BIBLIOGRAPHY

Anon., 'After a while you learn'.

Anon., 'Go to a tree'.

Anon., 'I have seen thee'.

Anon. Bulgarian proverb, 'God promises a safe landing'.

Aurelius, Marcus, *Meditations*, transl. Maxwell Staniforth. Penguin Classics, 1964.

Bach, Richard, *Illusions: The Adventures of a Reluctant Messiah*, Pan Books Ltd, 1978.

Bible: The Authorised Version.

Bible: New English Bible (2nd edn).

Bible: Revised Standard Version.

Blake, William, *The Poetical Works of William Blake*, Oxford University Press, 1913.

Blanding, Don, 'A Journey Ends', Source unknown.

Browning, Elizabeth Barrett, 'Aurora Leigh', *Aurora Leigh and Other Poems*, Women's Press, 1978.

Browning, Robert, 'Pippa Passes', *Poems*, Oxford University Press, 1949.

Caddy, Eileen, *The Living Word*, The Findhorn Press, 1977.

Emerson, Ralph Waldo, *Essays*, Dent, Everyman's Library, 1972.

Epictetus, *see* Marcus Aurelius.

Feild, Reshad, *A Travelling People's Feild Guide*, Element Books, 1986.

Gibran, Kahlil, *The Prophet*, William Heinemann Ltd, 1963.

Gibran, Kahlil, *Sand and Foam*, William Heinemann Ltd, 1927.

Grenfell, Joyce, *Joyce: by Herself and Her Friends*, Macmillan, 1980.

Gyatso, Geshe Kelsang, *Joyful Path and Good Fortune*, Tharpa Publications, London, 1990.

Haich, Elisabeth, *The Day with Yoga*. Aurora Press, Santa Fe, 1983.

Holland, Canon Henry Scott, passage attributed to.

Hopkins, Gerard Manley, 'Pied Beauty', *Poems*, Oxford University Press, 1970.

Julian of Norwich, *Revelations of Divine Love*, ed., Betty Radice, transl. Clifton Wolters, Penguin Classics, 1966.

Kübler-Ross, Elisabeth. Extracts from an interview with Elisabeth Kübler-Ross. *Kindred Spirit* Magazine, Foxhole, Dartington, Devon TQ9 6EB.

Lawrence, D. H., 'Shadows', *Complete Poems*, ed. Vivian De Sola Pinto and F. W. Roberts, Heinemann, 1972.

Mason, John, 'How Shall I Sing That Majesty?'. *The Methodist Hymn Book*. 1933.

Mello, Anthony de, *One Minute Wisdom*, Gujarat Sahitya Prakash, 1985.

Mello, Anthony de, *The Song of the Bird*, Image Books, 1984.

Morgan, The Reverend Daishin, *The Essential Teachings of Buddhism*, ed. Kerry Brown and Joanne O'Brien.

Newton, John, 'How Sweet the Name of Jesus Sounds'. *The Methodist Hymn Book*, 1933.

Penn, William, 'Some Fruits of Solitude', 1693. Source unknown.

Shakespeare, William, *As You Like It*.

Shakespeare, William, 'Shall I compare thee to a summer's day?', Sonnet XVIII.

Sitwell, Edith, 'Eurydice', *Collected Poems*, Macmillan, 1957.

Smith, Walter Chalmers, 'Immortal, invisible, God only wise'. *The Methodist Hymn Book*, 1933.

Stowe, Harriet Beecher, 'Still, still with Thee'. *The Methodist Hymn Book*, 1933.

Tagore, Rabindranath, *Sadhana*, Macmillan, 1913.

Tagore, Rabindranath, *Collected Poems and Plays of Rabindranath Tagore*, Macmillan, 1936.

Tiradhammo, Ajahn, *The Essential Teachings of Buddhism*, ed. Kerry Brown and Joanne O'Brien.

Torrie, Margaret, *Selected Poems*, 1979. Published in aid of the National Charity Cruse, founded 1959.

Trungpa, Chögyam, *Mudra*, Shambhala, 1972.

Van Dyke, Henry, 'They who tread the path of labour'.

Vaughan, Henry, 'The World', *Complete Poems*, ed. Alan Rudrum, Penguin, 1976.

Von Hugel, Freiderich, last words of.

Watts, Isaac, 'When I survey the wondrous cross'.

Whittier, John Greenleaf, 'Dear Lord and Father of mankind'.

Whittier, John Greenleaf, 'Immortal love for ever full'.

'Zed', from the teachings of 'Zed'.